Gratitude Journal

Journal

Finding joy in life's little things

created by

Theresa Flynn Gray

DIY Peaceful Living - Volume 1

Version 1/February 2018
Copyright © 2018 Theresa Flynn Gray
https://MoneyMatters.Life

Financial Fitness Logo by B-Hive Creative

DEDICATION

I dedicate my every day to God
and
to my wonderful family
Eric, Juliet and Wesley

^i^

I made this journal to help us all
find joy in every day.

in everything give

thanks

for this is the will of God in Christ Jesus for you.

1 Thessalonians 5:18

How to use this journal:

1. Every member of your family should have their own journal. Even little ones who cannot write yet can orally answer the questions (and someone can record their answers) or they can draw their own pictures.

2. Set the journals out at the dinner table a few times a week.

3. Take 5 minutes to have everyone answer <u>one</u> question.

4. Read the prompt on the left page and answer it on the right side page in the space provided. Be sure to date each entry!

5. Have each family member share their entries.

What were the nice things that people did for you this week?

Who gave you compliments this week?

date _____

date _____

What did you do
yesterday to show
kindness to
someone?

What happened
today that you
liked?

date _____

_____

_____

_____

_____

_____

date _____

_____

_____

_____

_____

_____

The people
in my life
who love me
are...

The people
that I love
are...

Date _____

Date _____

My favorite
nicknames are...

This week I was
kind to...

Date _____

Date _____

Draw a picture of something that makes you happy.

What are you grateful for today?

What happened yesterday that made you happy?

date _____

_____

_____

_____

_____

_____

date _____

_____

_____

_____

_____

_____

I was happy this week because I got to...

Things I am grateful to have in my house...

date _____

date _____

What gives you 'warm fuzzies'?

What did you learn today?

date _____

_____

_____

_____

_____

_____

date _____

_____

_____

_____

_____

_____

Draw a picture
of your home.

What happened
this week that
made you smile?

date _____

date _____

List your
favorite
hobbies.

What do you
know how to
do now that
was hard to
learn?

Date _____

_____

_____

_____

_____

_____

Date _____

_____

_____

_____

_____

_____

What were the best parts of today?

What happened this week that you are grateful for?

date _____

_____

_____

_____

_____

_____

date _____

_____

_____

_____

_____

_____

Draw a picture
of what you are
most thankful
for.

What happened yesterday that made you happy?

What were the best parts of today?

Who made your life a little happier today?

What happened this year that make you proud of yourself?

date _____

_____

_____

_____

_____

_____

date _____

_____

_____

_____

_____

_____

What clothes did you wear this week that you love?

Where did you get the clothes (from above)?

date _____

date _____

I am
grateful
for...

This week,
I was
thankful
that...

Date _____

Date _____

List 5 songs that make your heart sing.

Name the people who are your heroes.

What are you grateful for?

Who made you smile today?

What did you enjoy yesterday?

What are you grateful for this month?

date _____

_____

_____

_____

_____

_____

date _____

_____

_____

_____

_____

_____

Draw a picture of you with your family.

Name 5 people you are grateful for.

What were the best parts of today?

date _____

_____

_____

_____

_____

_____

date _____

_____

_____

_____

_____

_____

41

Draw a picture
of your
favorite
family memory.

Name 5
beautiful
things.

Who do you
know that
needs a
compliment
?

date _____

date _____

What are you grateful for today?

What happened yesterday that made you happy?

date _____

_____

_____

_____

_____

_____

date _____

_____

_____

_____

_____

_____

47

What are you grateful for?

Who made you smile today?

Draw a picture of yourself, smiling.

Who helped you this week?

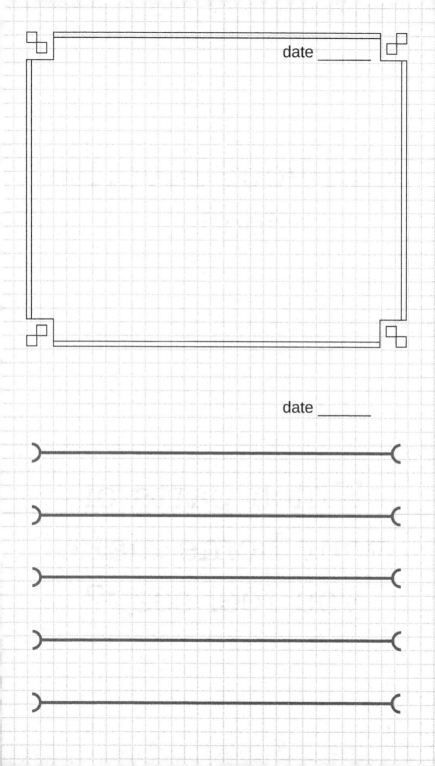

date _____

date _____

List your favorite foods.

Which parts of your home make you feel cozy?

date _____

_____

_____

_____

_____

_____

date _____

_____

_____

_____

_____

_____

Since this time last year, I have learned...

Since I woke up today, I...

Date _____

Date _____

When I grow up I want to be a...

Who do you know that does their job really well?

Date _____

Date _____

What are your talents?

What makes you unique?

What did you
learn from
your mistakes
this month?

How can
people tell
that you are
happy?

Date _____

_____

_____

_____

_____

Date _____

_____

_____

_____

_____

The names of the friends that make me happy...

I can show my family that I care for them by...

date _____

date _____

Draw a picture of you doing something that you love to do.

What are your favorite possessions?

Name 5 awesome things that happened last year.

Draw a picture of you and your friends.

Were you
happier today
or yesterday?
Draw a picture
of something
that makes you
happy.

Who made you
smile today?

date _____

date _____

What makes you smile?

What were you most grateful for this week?

Date _____

_____

_____

_____

_____

_____

Date _____

_____

_____

_____

_____

_____

What were the
nice things
that people did
for you this
week?

Who gave you
compliments
this week?

date _____

date _____

What did you do yesterday to show kindness to someone?

What happened today that you liked?

date _____

_____

_____

_____

_____

_____

date _____

_____

_____

_____

_____

_____

The people
in my life
who love me
are...

The people
that I love
are...

Date _____

Date _____

My favorite
nicknames are...

This week I was
kind to...

Date _____

~~~~~~~~~~~~~~~

~~~~~~~~~~~~~~~

~~~~~~~~~~~~~~~

~~~~~~~~~~~~~~~

~~~~~~~~~~~~~~~

Date _____

~~~~~~~~~~~~~~~

~~~~~~~~~~~~~~~

~~~~~~~~~~~~~~~

~~~~~~~~~~~~~~~

~~~~~~~~~~~~~~~

Draw a picture of something that makes you happy.

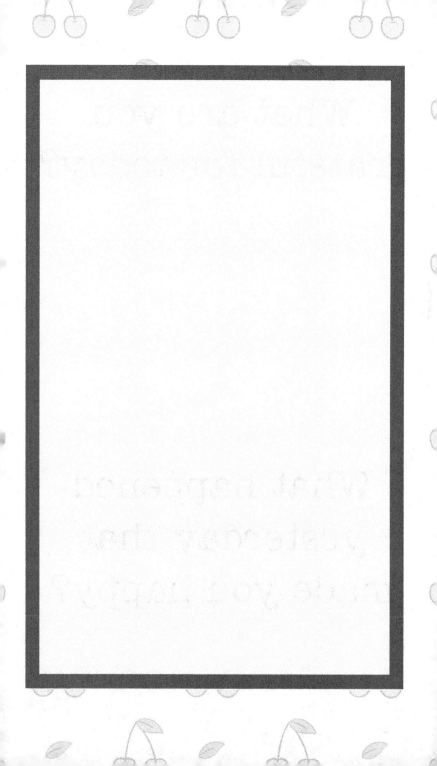

What are you grateful for today?

What happened yesterday that made you happy?

date _____

_____

_____

_____

_____

_____

date _____

_____

_____

_____

_____

_____

I was happy this week because I got to...

Things I am grateful to have in my house...

date _____

date _____

What gives you 'warm fuzzies'?

What did you learn today?

date _____

_____

_____

_____

_____

_____

date _____

_____

_____

_____

_____

_____

Draw a picture
of your home.

What happened
this week that
made you smile?

date _____

date _____

List your
favorite
hobbies.

What do you
know how to
do now that
was hard to
learn?

Date _____

_____

_____

_____

_____

_____

Date _____

_____

_____

_____

_____

_____

Draw a picture of what you are most thankful for.

What were the best parts of today?

What happened this week that you are grateful for?

date _____

_____

_____

_____

_____

_____

date _____

_____

_____

_____

_____

_____

What happened yesterday that made you happy?

What were the best parts of today?

Who made your
life a little
happier today?

What happened
this year that
make you proud
of yourself?

date _____

_____

_____

_____

_____

_____

date _____

_____

_____

_____

_____

_____

What clothes
did you wear
this week that
you love?

Where did you
get the clothes
(from above)?

date _____

date _____

I am grateful for...

This week, I was thankful that...

Date _____

Date _____

List 5 songs that make your heart sing.

Name the people who are your heroes.

Date _____

Date _____

What are you grateful for?

Who made you smile today?

date _____

date _____

What did you enjoy yesterday?

What are you grateful for this month?

date _____

_____

_____

_____

_____

_____

date _____

_____

_____

_____

_____

_____

Draw a picture of you with your family.

Name 5 people you are grateful for.

What were the best parts of today?

date _____

_____

_____

_____

_____

_____

date _____

_____

_____

_____

_____

_____

Draw a picture
of your
favorite
family memory.

Name 5 beautiful things.

Who do you know that needs a compliment?

Draw a picture of you doing something that you love to do.

What are your favorite possessions?

Name 5 awesome things that happened last year.

Rejoice in the Lord always.

I will say it again: Rejoice!

Let your gentleness be evident to all.

The Lord is near.

Do not be anxious about anything,

but in every situation,

by prayer and petition,

with thanksgiving,

present your requests to God.

And the peace of God,

which transcends all understanding,

will guard your hearts and your minds in Christ Jesus.

-Philippians 4:4-7

thanks

Thank you for using this journal!

Please email me with any thoughts
you have or any suggestions for
future volumes!

Theresa@MoneyMatters.Life